Selling Your Book the Easy Way

Learn How to Write a Great Book Proposal in 7 Days.

from the files of the
Thrive Learning Institute

Table of Contents

LEGAL NOTICE

The Publisher has striven to be as accurate and complete as possible in the creation of this report, notwithstanding the fact that he does not warrant or represent at any time that the contents within are accurate due to the rapidly changing nature of the Internet.

While all attempts have been made to verify information provided in this publication, the Publisher assumes no responsibility for errors, omissions, or contrary interpretation of the subject matter herein. Any perceived slights of specific persons, peoples, or organizations are unintentional.

In practical advice books, like anything else in life, there are no guarantees of income made. Readers are cautioned to reply on their own judgment about their individual circumstances to act accordingly.

This book is not intended for use as a source of legal, business, accounting or financial advice. All readers are advised to seek services of competent professionals in legal, business, accounting, and finance field.

Bonus

Get No-Charge Access to Writing and Publishing Materials from Our Library Collection

Instant Access - Join Here

Click or type into your browser:

http://livesensical.com/go/writingbooks/

Introduction

Sell your book the easy way - write a proposal

You can get paid to write a book. It's easily possible to make a fast $10,000, or even a six figure amount. You could even make seven figures --- over a million dollars for twenty pages of text. It sounds incredible, but a fast seven figures is certainly possible if you have a HOT, hot idea or have had an experience that hundreds of thousands of people want to read about. In his 2001 book about writing non-fiction, "Damn! Why Didn't I Write That?", author Marc McCutcheon says that it's not hard to make a good income: "you can learn the trade and begin making a respectable income much faster than most people think possible".

The good part is that you don't need to write your book before you get some money. You write a proposal, and a publisher will give you an advance, which you can live on while you write the book.

Writing a proposal is the smart way to write a book. It's the way professional writers sell non-fiction. Selling a book on a proposal is much easier than selling a book that you've already written. A book proposal is a complete description of your book. It contains the title, an explanation of what the book's about, an outline of chapters, a market and competition survey, and a sample chapter.

A book proposal functions in the same way as any business proposal does: you're making an offer to someone you hope to do business with. It will be treated by publishers in the same way that any business treats a proposal. A publisher will read your proposal, assess its feasibility, cost it, and if it looks as if the publisher will make money, the publisher will pay you to write the book. When you've sold your proposed book to a publisher, your role doesn't end with writing your book. You're in partnership with your publisher to ensure the book's success. If you do your part, both you and your publisher will make money.

You and your publisher: a partnership

The publisher's business is selling books. The company acquires books which it hopes will sell, and sell well. Your publisher is putting up the money to publish your book, so you need to approach the project from his point of view as well as your own.

We haven't got the space to go into great detail about the publishing business here, but you need to know about "returns", because the challenge of returns makes publishing different from other businesses. Publishers sell books on consignment. Publishers ship books to bookshops, and if a book isn't sold within a certain time period, it's destroyed. The bookseller strips the cover from the book and sends the cover to the publisher for a full credit. This is the "return". If a title doesn't sell, the publisher takes a beating. As you can imagine, publishers are no more keen to lose money than you or I.

What does this mean to you as you write your book proposal? It means that your proposal needs to emphasize the ways in which you, as the writer, will take responsibility for the book's success.

You will try to ensure the success of your book by gauging the marketplace. You will work out who the likely buyers of your book might be, and the reasons they will have for paying good money for your book. You'll assess the competition for your book. You'll work out ways in which you can promote your book, so that people hear about it. You're in partnership with your publisher, and if you're prepared to take responsibility for that role, the publisher will be much more likely to buy your proposal.

Why write a proposal first?

All non-fiction books are sold on proposal. A book proposal is much easier to sell than a complete book.

Here are some of the reasons:

- It's easier to read a 20 or 30 page proposal than a 400 page book;
- It's easier to make changes in the book's concept at the proposal stage;
- With a proposal, the publisher, in the person of your editor, can take ownership of the book. It's like bespoke tailoring: the editor feels that the book has been specifically written for the publishing house.

Even if you decide to write your book first, you'll need to create a proposal once you've written it. No agent or publisher is interested in reading an entire book to assess its viability. That's the proposal's job:

to ensure that your book has a niche in the marketplace. As you do your research for the proposal, you'll work out whether or not your book is likely to sell. You can shape the book at the proposal stage, much more easily than you can when it's a huge stack of print or a giant computer file.

Sometimes you may get an idea for a book, but the idea is amorphous, it doesn't have a real shape. You may want to write several thousand words to see whether the book becomes clearer in your mind. But write the proposal before you write more than ten thousand words, because your book must target a specific group of buyers.

How do you write a book proposal?

You write a proposal step by step. In this ebook, we'll work on your book proposal together. Each chapter has tasks for you to complete. Once you've completed all the tasks, you'll have a book proposal which has an excellent chance of selling.

Here's what we'll cover:

- ✓ (Day One) Getting an idea for your book.

- ✓ (Day Two) Developing the idea and expanding on it. Assessing the market. Who needs this book? What's the competition for the book?

- ✓ (Day Three) Writing the blurb. Outlining your book.

- ✓ (Day Four) Researching your book proposal, and fleshing out your outline.

- ✓ (Day Five) Writing a proposal query letter. Sending your query letters to agents and publishers. (You send the queries while you're working on the proposal. This helps you to gauge reaction to your work.)

- ✓ (Day Six) Writing the proposal.

- ✓ (Day Seven) Writing the sample chapter. Revising your proposal.

I'll be including a sample of a book proposal for you to look at, so you can see what material the proposal contains. This proposal garnered an agent contract the first time I sent it out. I'll also include other samples, so that you have plenty of templates from which to construct your own proposal.

How to use this ebook

First, read through the book, to see what information it contains.

Next, work through the book, chapter by chapter. As you read each chapter, do the tasks and the exercises in the order in which they appear. Doing them will help you to write not just one, but many book proposals. Remember, the primary aim of this book is to help you write your first book proposal and be well on the way to selling it by the time you've worked your way through all the chapters.

Work FAST

It's vital that you concentrate on getting the words down on paper. As long as you have something on paper you can fix it. As we work through the material, I'll be encouraging you to work FAST and not think to much about what you're writing. Thinking has no business in your first draft. Thinking comes later as you rewrite.

Can't devote a week to writing your proposal?

If you're on vacation you can set aside a couple of weeks to work on your proposal. But what if you don't have a vacation due? Easy! You can fit writing into your busy life. You'll still follow all the steps, but it will take you longer. Try to stick to a set schedule. You may decide that you'll complete a chapter a week, for example.

Work fast. Work on your book proposal EVERY DAY, even if you only have five minutes to spare. This is because at the beginning, ideas are fragile. Time spent with your proposal each day helps you to build and maintain your energy and your enthusiasm.

Day One: What's a book proposal? Get an idea for your book

Day One Tasks

Task One: Look over four non-fiction books

Take your notebook and visit a bookstore. Skim four non-fiction books of the kind which you hope to write. Check the number of pages, the table of contents, and chapter length. How are these books written? Are they written in a casual, tongue-in-cheek style like the For Dummies series? Do they include lots of anecdotes and personal information about the author?

In your notebook, write down each book's title, author, publisher and year of publication. Also write down anything you find interesting about the book. Scan the acknowledgements page to see whether the author thanks her editor and her agent. Make a note of their names if she does. (These people may be interested in your proposal if it covers a similar subject area.)

Task Two: Work through the Idea Generator exercises in this chapter

Read the Idea Generators, and do at least three of them, even if you've already got an idea for your book. Working through this material is important because it will give you confidence that you it's easy for you to find as many ideas as you need.

Task Three: Create a computer folder to hold your working files

Create a folder on your computer to hold all the files for your book. As you work, you'll generate many files. Create sub-folders as you need them.

Task Four: Create a Work Log

Create a file on your computer as a diary for this project. Paste all the information you gather while searching the Internet and while communicating with others in this log. Date each entry. If you need to leave your project for a few days, you can read your log to get back into the groove of your project.

What's a book proposal?

A book proposal is a business document which convinces a publisher to buy your book before you've written it. Your proposal says, in effect: "Hey, I've got a great idea for a book which lots of people will want to buy. Do you want to publish it?"

Think of it as a combination brochure and outline of your proposed book.

There's a standard format of material that your book proposal will need to cover. This doesn't mean that you need to hew completely to this format. It's just a guideline of topics your proposal must contain.

Your book proposal must contain:

- A title page, with the title, subtitle, author, word count of the completed book, and estimated time frame for completion. You might state: "75,000 words, completion three months after agreement".

- An overview: a description of the book. This can be as short as a paragraph, or several pages long.

- The background of the author. Your biography, as it relates to your expertise for this book.

- The competition in the marketplace. This is where you mention the top four or five titles which are your book's competitors. (Note: if there are dozens of competitors for your book, this is a good thing, because it means that the subject area is popular. Your book will need to take a new slant.)

- Promotions. This is where you describe how you will promote your book, both before and after publication.

- A chapter outline.

- A sample chapter, or two chapters. This is always the first chapter, and if you're sending two chapters, it's the Introduction and Chapter One, or if there's no Introduction, it's Chapters One and Two.

- Attachments. Optional. You may want to attach articles you've written about the book's topic, or any relevant supporting material.

Got an idea for your book? Great!

If you already have an idea for your book, that's great. Please work through the material in this chapter using your current idea, or join us in developing new ideas. Open a new computer file so that you can work through the exercises as we progress.

Start here to develop an idea for your next book

There's nothing mysterious about coming up with ideas. Within a page or two, you'll have more ideas than you know what to do with. Your ideas start with YOU. When you think about what you enjoy, about your past experiences and your knowledge, you're guaranteed a regular fountain of ideas. Let's turn on the fountain.

As you do the following exercises, work through them quickly. Don't allow yourself to bog down. Do them as quickly as you can, and then go and do something else for a few hours, to let the ideas gestate and bubble in your subconscious mind.

When you come back, read through the ideas you generated, and add to them as you read through your lists. Please don't discard any ideas at this stage. This is because the way to a brilliant, fantastic idea is by twisting an idea slightly, reversing it, or by combining several ideas into a new one.

Searching for ideas alerts your subconscious mind that ideas are important to you. Over the next few days, you may get a nudge from an idea which says: "Write me down". Do that right away, even if you're in the middle of a shower or you're driving along the freeway. (If you're driving, pull over.) Write that idea down, because even if you're one hundred per cent certain that you will never in this lifetime forget that amazing idea you just had, believe me, you will forget it. Write it down, always.

When you stay alert to the idea hovering at the corners of your consciousness you will never be without a book bubbling away. This is how you turn your first book into a long series of books.

First thing in the morning is a great time to generate ideas. Set your alarm ten minutes early, then sit up in bed and jot down 50 ideas.

Idea Generator One: What you're good at

Make a list of 20 things you're good at. Don't think too hard about this. Maybe you're good at buying presents for people—you've got a knack for choosing just the right gift. Maybe you're a good cook, or a good parent, or a good swimmer or a good tennis player. Or maybe you used to be good at one or more of these things. For example: I grew up with horses, and owned horses for many years. I'm good with horses, and a good rider. If I saw a gap in the market for a horse book, I'd feel comfortable writing the book.

You get the idea. List at least 20 things that you're good at, or have been good at in the past. For example, if you know you're an excellent gardener, even though you now live an apartment, list "gardening".

Idea Generator Two: Your past experiences

Experiences sell. If you've been abducted by little green men from Mars, it's a book. If you're a bigamist, it's a book. People have written books about their illnesses (see from challenge to opportunity below), their addictions, and their pets. Browse through the bestseller lists to see what personal experiences people are writing about.

Here's where you walk down memory lane. If you're in your twenties, it'll be a short stroll. If you're in your forties or older, it will be a hike. Don't get bogged down with this, list 20 experiences you've had that spring to mind.

The easiest way to come up with experiences is to work backwards through the stages of your life, or through decades. Again, don't take a long time over this. Set yourself a time limit --- ten minutes is enough.

Idea Generator Three: Your knowledge

What do you know? Start by making a list of all the subjects you were good at in school. Then list all the jobs you've had – yes, part time work counts.

Also list:

- Your hobbies. Are you a keen Chihuahua breeder? Do you quilt? Take photographs?

- Your current job. What are you learning in your job that other people would pay to learn?

- The places you've lived. Your hometown may be boring to you, but guide books sell well.

- Your family tree. What special knowledge do your nearest and dearest have that you could write about?

Spend around ten minutes writing down as many subjects as you have knowledge about.

Idea Generator Four: What you enjoy most

Celebrity chef Nigella Lawson freely admits that she cooks because she loves to eat. Nigella has turned her love of food into a career. She regularly produces bestselling books. (Her chocolate recipes are brilliant.) What do you love? People have written about garage sales, cosmetics, cars, vacations. If you love something, chances are that thousands or maybe millions of others will love it too.

Watch the newspapers and take note of current trends. Or better yet, listen to what your children are talking about, or asking you to buy for them. Children tend to be well up on what's happening.

Remember that it will take around two years for your book to reach the bookstores. Therefore, the currently hot topics on the bestselling lists may be old news before your book is in the stores. This doesn't mean of course that you can't write on perennial favourites like money, sex and exercise. These topics never go out of popularity, and a new twist on one of these is always a sure bet.

The idea of writing about what you enjoy is that you will be bringing passion and enthusiasm to your topic. Enthusiasm is a must.

Idea Generator Five: From challenge to opportunity

You face challenges every day. Most are minor, some are major challenges. If you've ever faced a large challenge, or if you're facing one right now, then consider that the things you learn could help other people. Whatever your challenge is, whether it's moving house or confronting a life-threatening illness, other people face the same challenges, and in those challenges lie the seeds of books.

Make a list of 20 challenges you've faced in your life. Anything catastrophic qualifies: losing your job, facing bankruptcy, the betrayal of a spouse. If you've had a quiet life, then make a list of challenges that the people you know have faced.

Additional challenges you can consider include any habit you've broken, from congenital lateness to overeating.

When you've finished brainstorming, you'll have dozens of book ideas. Winnow out the non-starters. Don't delete them, move them to another computer file. Call it "odds and ends" or "snippets".

Checklist: Is this the right idea for you TODAY?

You've worked through the idea generators, and you have one or more ideas which you feel would work as a book. The next step is to scrutinize your primary idea carefully.

Consider your idea and look at this list of questions. See if you can answer "Yes" to all of them:

1. Am I enthusiastic enough about this subject and my ideas about it to sell this proposal to an agent and an editor – and to readers?

2. Will I retain my enthusiasm through the months it will take me to complete the book?

3. Is there a market for my book? (I've checked Amazon.com and bookshops for competing titles. I'm convinced there is a market for my book.)

4. I can find people with expert knowledge to interview as I write my book.

5. Does my book provide solutions to problems?

If you can answer YES to most of these questions, you're set. Great! We're going to start work on your proposal.

Day Two: Develop your idea and assess the market

Day Two Tasks

Task One: Keep studying non-fiction books

The more you know about how non-fiction books are constructed the more easily you'll be able to work on your own book with confidence. Look at the books on your shelves at home, and at your local library. (Be sure to make a note of any editor or agent acknowledgements.)

Task Two: Develop your idea

Work through the various steps in developing your idea. (See "Simple Steps In Developing Your Idea" in this chapter.

Dispelling myths and a word about confidence

If you're feeling nervous now that you're about to start this project, relax. Tell yourself that you will take it step by step. All you need to do is work at it steadily, a word, sentence and paragraph at a time, and you will complete your proposal, and then when you've sold the proposal, you'll complete your book using the same easy-does-it method.

While we're at it, let's dispel a few myths.

Myth One - It takes a special talent to write books.

It takes persistence. There are as many different kinds of writers as there are people. Some are young, some are elderly, many are in-between. You don't need any special writing talent to write books, nor do you need to be highly educated. Many successful writers have never completed high school. If you can write well enough to write a letter, you can write a book.

Myth Two - Writers starve in garrets.

Many professional writers make incomes that would make doctors and lawyers envious. Most make reasonable incomes. If you decide to make a career of writing non-fiction books, the major benefit is that if you choose your book's topic with care, your book can stay in print for many years. For each year that your book's in print, you get two royalty checks. Let's say that you write two books a year for five years. At the end of the five years, if your books all stay in print, you'll be getting ten royalty checks a year. These ongoing royalties are your nest-egg, profitable investments in your future.

Myth Three - It's hard to sell a book.

As long as you research the market for each book before you write as much as a single word, it's easy to sell a book. Publishers need competent, reliable writers who can produce good books regularly. This myth got started because --- let's be blunt here--- 99 per cent of submissions to editors and publishers are not publishable.

Myth Four - You need to know someone to get a book published.

You need to write a good book to get a book published. That really is all you need to do. I started writing romance novels and they were published by an English publisher. I certainly didn't know anyone in UK publishing; I live in Australia. If you have a contact in publishing, by all means use that contact. However, it's not necessary. Publishing is big business, and publishers need good books.

Today we'll develop your idea and assess the market

Developing your idea and assessing the market go together. We'll work on both tasks today. The idea of working on both tasks together is that as you read through the outlines of books which cover a similar area to yours, you'll see what's already been published, and you'll get fresh ideas for material that you can cover in your own book.

Note: your personal experience is valuable

As you skim through other people's books, jot down any thoughts and ideas you get. You should make a note of any experiences you remember which you could include in your book. This is because everyone loves a story, so no matter what subject area your book covers, include your own anecdotes. If you're writing a diet book, include funny/ informative stories about your own experiences with diets, or the experiences of your friends.

You may want to use fictitious names to protect people's privacy. You will definitely need to use fictitious names if you can't contact people to ask for permission to use a story or if you think there's a chance that people will be able to recognize themselves from a story you tell that puts them in a bad light.

For example, perhaps you belonged to a group of dieters, and you tell a story about another person in the group. Even if this was 20 years ago, and you've given this person a fictitious name, disguise the story: change the person's sex, age, and occupation.

Simple steps in developing your idea

Work on developing your idea step by step. Here's how:

1. Write down everything you know about this idea

Let's say you've decided to write a book on natural healthcare for pets. You own several dogs and a cat, and are an enthusiast for natural healthcare because it's worked for you and for your friends. Today you're going to make copious notes. You're going to write down everything you can think of which relates to your idea. It doesn't matter whether you use a computer file, or a pen and paper, sit down and get ready.

Ask yourself: who, what, how, when, where and why. Make topic headings for each question. Then answer each question. Don't try to write in complete sentences, just make notes. For example, if you took one of your dogs to a doggie chiropractor for several years, note down the chiropractor's name, the dog's name, problems the dog had, the number of sessions --- anything and everything you can remember. Also write down what you don't know, so you can find out. (One of the benefits of research is that you get to answer all the questions you have about a topic.)

Take as much time as you need. You may want to work in forty-minute sessions, and then go and do something else for a while. Taking breaks is important. It's during the breaks that your subconscious mind will go to work for you can scan your memory banks to come up with more ideas.

Don't discard any of your ideas. And write down every idea, no matter how tangential. Your mind works via associations. Therefore, if you get a notion to write down "Phips --- broken leg" write this down, even if it seems that it has nothing to do with natural healthcare for pets. Phips was your first dog, and was hit by a car. This was 30 years ago, and you don't remember much about the incident. However, after writing it down, you ask your mother about Phips, and she tells you that the little Corgi was bred by a woman who was into natural healthcare (you didn't remember this --- you may not even have known it, but somehow your subconscious got you to write it down). You contact the woman, who's elderly, but who's a fountain of useful information, and she provides almost a chapter of information for your book. You'll find that you have many serendipitous incidents like this as you write your proposal and your book.

2. Make a long list of possible book titles

At this stage, you don't need the perfect title, Healthcare for Pets will do as your working title. Make a list of 20 title ideas as quickly as you can. (And save the list.)

Don't sweat a title. You'll often find that the perfect title doesn't occur to you until you book is completely written. Or, your publisher may come up with a title they want to use.

3. Create a list of contacts

Who could help you with information for this book? Write down the name of everyone you can think of. Do this quickly, you can look up their email address or postal address when the time comes to contact them. At this stage, you just want a list of all those people who will be able to help you.

Is there an association of people who might help? In our Healthcare for Pets example, there will be numerous veterinary associations and kennel club associations of people who could provide valuable information.

Create an Acknowledgements computer file. Whenever someone helps you with information for the book, type their name into the Acknowledgements file. People get a kick out of helping an author with a book, and the best way to thank them is to make sure that their name appears on the Acknowledgements page in the book.

Assess the market for your book

1. Visit large bookstores

Start by visiting some large bookstores. Take your notebook and a pen. Copy the Tables of Contents of books that treat the same subject matter that your book does. You will want to make your book significantly different from other books which cover the same topic. If your book is exactly the same as other books on the topic, no publisher will be interested in buying it. However, you shouldn't be discouraged if there are many books covering the area which you intend to cover. Lots of books mean that this area is very popular. For example, publishers bring out dozens of diet books each year. And there's room for yours, too!

Aim for at least three to five points of difference. This doesn't mean that you have to come up with all new information. In fact, presenting completely new information is impossible. Sticking with our diet book example, there's only one way to lose weight, and that's to take in fewer calories than you expend. Authors reveal this ghastly news to their readers in many ways. Therefore, it's how you present the material that counts. If you can show readers a new way to diet, and you can prove that your method works, you're in, with a hot seller on your hands.

2. Visit your library

Next, drive to the library. Ask the librarian for Books In Print. This is a multi-volume set of reference books which lists all the books currently available by author, subject and title. Your library may have the books, or it may have the BIP CDs. If your library's BIP is on CD, get a printout of all the books in your subject area.

Don't faint if you see an ultra-lengthy list! Several years ago when I was assessing the market for a book on time management, BIP spat out ten-plus pages. I got all the books which sounded as though they might be similar via inter-library loan, and none resembled my book at all. So the fact that there are lots and lots of books means little other than that this subject is popular. This is a good thing!

Next check out Forthcoming Books. FC should be available at your library right near BIP. FC lists all those books which will be released in the next six months.

You'll want to have the books which are the main competition for your book on hand if possible. You don't have to buy them all. You can borrow them from the library, or if they're listed on Amazon.com, you can use Amazon.com's clever "Look Inside" technology, so that you can scan the contents pages of competing titles.

3. Amazon.com

Amazon.com is your next port of call. Type the subject of your book into the search query box, and you'll get a list of all those books which touch on your subject area. Print out this list. Having the list handy helps you when the time comes to pick a title.

Read the descriptions, and all the reviews of any books which sound as if they might be similar to yours.

Write a report on your discoveries

Now you've finished surveying the marketplace as it stands for your idea, take the time to write a brief report on what you've discovered. This report is for your own use. Do this right away when it's all still fresh in your mind. It's important to do this, because when you talk to your editor or agent, you'll want to have all the information on the market situation handy. Your report doesn't have to be long. A page will do.

Day Three: Write the blurb and outline your book

Day Three Tasks

Task One: Write at least three blurbs

Write at least three blurbs for your book: 200 words, 50 words, and 25 words. (See the sample blurbs in this chapter.)

Task Two: Collect sample blurbs

Blurbs sell books. Everyone from the publisher who initially buys the proposal, to the book store owner who stocks your book will decide whether they're interested in your book based on the blurb alone.

Become a connoisseur of blurbs. Start your own blurb collection. Each time you see a blurb which you think is effective, copy it, and put it into your Blurb File.

Writing the blurb

The "blurb" is the back cover material for your book --- the selling points which will get people to buy the book. If you write the blurb before you write an outline, you're guaranteed not to wander off the track as you write your book.

I can't emphasize the importance of your blurb enough. If you've been thinking of skipping this section, please don't. Here are some reasons to write your blurb first:

- it keeps you focused on the theme of your book;

- it makes writing the outline easier;

- it makes selling your proposal easier;

- it will assure your agent and editor that you know what you're doing, and they'll feel comfortable working with you and handing over the advance;

- when you've sold the book, and the time comes to write it, you'll have an easier time because you can keep the blurb at the forefront of your mind.

Your blurb helps your agent and editor to get a contract for you

Your blurb is the "sales story" for your book. If your agent becomes enthusiastic about your book, she'll become enthusiastic on the basis of your blurb. She'll use the blurb as her sales pitch to other people. For example, when she talks to an editor at a publishing house who may be interested in your book, she'll start with your blurb. The conversation will stop there if the editor doesn't see the book's potential. Let's say that the editor likes the blurb enough to look at the proposal. If she's still keen, it's her turn to sell your book, on the basis of the blurb, to the other people in the publishing company. She'll need to convince Sales and Marketing that they can sell your book. If they're not keen, you won't get an offer.

When you've written your book, your publisher will try to sell your book to book distributors, and later to booksellers, all on the basis of the blurb that you started out with. So the time that you spend working on the blurb is not wasted, it's the most important part of your book. Without a good blurb, your book will not come into existence.

Having said all that, it's also important that you don't obsess over your blurb. Everything you write can be fixed, so focus on getting your blurb written, in various lengths, rather than striving to make your blurb perfect. Your blurb may well go through many incarnations: you'll make changes, your agent may want changes, and your editors will definitely want changes.

Sample blurbs

Here are two sample blurbs.

The first is from one of my earlier books, published by a major publishing company in 1997. I wrote this blurb while I was working to gather material for the book. It took me around ten minutes to write. You'll often find that as you're starting to work on book, your blurb will come to you as a flash of inspiration. If it doesn't, don't worry about it, just follow the process outlined below.

Sample blurb from: [Title Excerpted] by Beau Tighe

You're about to meet a very powerful genie. This genie will give you all the time you need to be everything you want to be, to do everything you want to do, and to have everything you want to have --- you are this genie!

[Title Excerpted] shows you how to manage your time so that you can achieve any goals you set for yourself. You'll learn to feel focused and relaxed as you achieve your goals.

Spend 21 days with [Title Excerpted] and in just 20 minutes a day you'll learn to how to:

- Focus, so that you get more done in less time;

- Separate tasks into the urgent and the important;

- Effectively prioritise and delegate tasks;

- Practise relaxation daily until it becomes a habit;

- Determine your values, so that you can set appropriate goals;

- And become more creative.

Each day's reading will give you ideas, inspiration and motivation, as well as simple tasks to help you develop your time management skills.

(The above blurb is around 200 words. Create several versions of your blurb at different lengths --- more on this below.)

The second is from another book which was published in 1998. I didn't write this blurb until the book was complete, and the publisher was sending a brief to the cover designer. This blurb took me a long time to write. I also had a lot of trouble writing the book, and I think that if I'd written the blurb before I started, I would have had a much easier time with the book, and would have enjoyed writing it more.

Sample blurb from: [Title Excerpted] by Beau Tighe

When you use the Internet for your business you don't need to wait for customers to come to you because a Web site is a 24-hour sales force to the whole world. [Title Excerpted] offers clear and practical advice on how to use the Internet to develop your business; how to promote your products and services; how to find vital information; and how to pursue new business opportunities.

This book includes the following features:

- Introduces online basics and describes the equipment you will need to get your business online and build your own Web site;

- Offers practical advice on how to expand your business online, including tips on your site's useability, how to market your Web site, and how to boost Internet sales;

- Provides case studies of how people are using the Internet inexpensively and simply to develop their businesses;

- Includes a fast-finder directory of useful resources available to businesses on the Internet: company contacts and suppliers; trainers and educators; financial sites; government and legal information; human resources; freebies on the Internet; and other SOHO-related resources.

By using the Internet you can run more business more efficiently with lowered costs, fewer staff, and less space requirement, and have more time to develop your business creatively. Explore the advantages to your business of e-commerce using your Web site as a merchant commerce system that can handle orders, payment and fulfilment via the site.

The above blurb runs to almost 250 words, which is a little long. If I were writing the book now, I would make it shorter and punchier.

The one-sentence version of the blurb is: "[Title Excerpted] offers clear and practical advice on how to use the Internet to develop your business; how to promote your products and services; how to find vital information; and how to pursue new business opportunities."

Write your blurb in easy steps

Before you start writing your blurb, ask yourself: who will be reading this book? This question is important, because it helps you to picture the reader as you write. Once you have an image of your ideal reader in your mind, you'll find it's much easier to work on your book. Working out who your readers will be also gives you a head start in writing the marketing section of your book proposal.

Let's stay with the book on natural healthcare for pets. Who would be interested in this book? Make a list. Your list could start with: pet owners who use natural healthcare, companies that manufacture natural petcare products, and veterinary surgeons.

Then go on and create your blurb in the following easy steps.

One: Make a list of the benefits to the reader

Your reader will buy the book because of the benefits the book gives her. Features are different from benefits. For example, you may be presenting recipes for making pet remedies. The pet remedies is a feature. The benefit of the pet remedies could be that they save the reader trips to the vet and money on expensive commercial products. YOU MUST USE THE BENEFITS IN YOUR BLURB.

First list all of the features your book will contain. Then make a list of all the benefits.

Take down three or four books from your shelves, and study their blurbs. Do they list the benefits? How are the benefits presented?

(You'll occasionally find that the author and publisher, not to mention the publisher's sales and marketing departments, were all asleep when the book was in production, and the blurb contains a long list of features. Work out how you'd convert those features into benefits. This is excellent practise for you.)

Two: Rank the benefits

Rank the benefits in their order of importance. You may want to get some help here. Read your list of benefits to a friend, and ask how she'd rank them.

Three: Write several blurbs, in various lengths

In addition to your list of benefits, your blurb can contain an intriguing fact, or a short anecdote. For example, if you once saved the life of your pet with a natural healthcare remedy, you could tell this story as part of your blurb.

When you've completed your blurb, in around 200 to 300 words, create shorter versions. Create one of 100 words, another of 50 words, and you can even try to pare it down to 25 words.

Here's a one sentence version of the sample blurb for LifeTime: "LifeTime: Better Time Management in 21 Days shows you how to manage your time so that you can achieve any goals you set for yourself." As you can see, the sentence is taken from the longer blurb.

Essential blurb add-on: the testimonial

Publishers love cover testimonials, because they know that they sell books. How many times have you bought a book because someone you'd heard of and respected recommended the book to you? If you know anyone famous, or can get in touch with them, now's the time to contact them to ask them whether they'd be willing to read your book and provide a quote for you to use on the cover.

Outlining your book

Start with a mind map

This is where your blurb comes into its own. You can develop a basic outline from your blurb as a mind map, or cluster diagram. For each book I've written, I've used mind maps. Because a book is long, it's hard to keep the whole thing straight in your mind --- mind maps help you to do this.

Diagramming your initial ideas of what you'd like the book to contain gives you an overview, from which you can develop a more detailed outline. Go through all the material you've gathered so far, and insert headings into your mind map.

Remember that at this stage, nothing is set in stone. Just work as quickly as you can, don't think too much about it. You just want to get an idea of how much material you have.

Create your outline

Working from your mind map, create a chapter outline of your book. The easiest way to do this is just to write numbers from one to ten or one to 15 down the page, and type in chapter headings. Most books have around ten to 15 chapters. If yours has more than 15, that's fine.

Only got three or four headings? No matter how little material you have, or how much, don't worry. This is the initial stages, remember. Just work quickly so that you get something down on paper. Tomorrow we'll be researching your book, and as you research, you're sure to find many more headings for your outline.

In these very early stages of working on your proposal, your subconscious mind is your greatest resource. Therefore, if you get an impulse to write down something, write it down, even if it doesn't make much sense to you. The reason you got this idea will come to you.

Day Four: Research your book proposal, and flesh out your book's outline

Day Four Tasks

Task One: Create your research plan

It's a good idea to create a research plan to guide you, both in writing your proposal, and later in writing your book. Knowing that you can find all the information you need is a confidence-builder.

Task Two: Create a chapter outline for your book

Write a chapter outline for your book proposal.

Research: How much do you need to know?

Remember that this is just a proposal, you're not writing the complete book. Therefore, you may not need to do any research at all. You may have all the material you need. If this is the case, you can go right on to fleshing out your outline.

If you need to gather material, then first you should develop a research plan. This may take you an hour or two, but it's time well spent. You will use this plan first to develop your proposal, and later when you're writing your book. For your proposal, you probably won't need to go past # 6 in your plan to get all the information you need.

Your research plan

1. Develop a frame of reference, and write it down as a complete sentence, using no more than 25 words. The shortest blurb you wrote should work well for this step.

2. Next, mind map or outline everything you need to research. This is to give you a quick overview. It's a good idea to print this mind map out so that you can glance at it as you work. You'll find that if you're online, or at the library, it's tempting to explore other avenues. These avenues may well be productive, and you can explore them at some stage, but not while you're trying to write your proposal. Once you start writing, your only goal should be: "get it done".

3. Do a general search on the Web using a search engine like Google.com to locate additional areas you could explore.

4. If you find mention of any online groups or mailing lists which seem appropriate for your subject, join them. The members may be able to provide you with anecdotes or other information.

5. Make a note of companies which are mentioned in your Web search. Can they help you? The benefit of asking companies to help you in your research is free, current information. Most companies will be only too pleased to help, for the PR boost you can give them. Make a note to yourself to acknowledge them in your book. If any company has given you a lot of help, it's a nice gesture to send them a copy when the book's published.

6. Check periodical indices for articles which might be useful. Once you needed to trudge along to the library for this kind of help, but LexisNexis (http://www.lexis.com/) is faster.

7. Are there any books which could help you? Try www.amazon.com to find recent books on your topic. (You may already have notes on these books which you collected while you were trying to come up with an idea for a book.)

8. Original sources. This is where your list of contacts comes in useful. Make a note of people you will want to interview, first for your proposal, and later, for your book.

9. Experts and organizations.

STOP! Don't collect more information than you need to write your proposal

Creating your research plan shouldn't take you more than an hour, or two hours maximum. Until you get into the writing process, whether it's your proposal, or the book itself, you won't know exactly what you need. As long as you have sufficient material for that day's work, you've got enough information.

Work on your book's outline and the first chapter, as you research

We'll do more work on the outline and first chapter later this week. But, because they form such a big part of your proposal, start working on them now, as you research.

The Brain-Dead Process

Here's a process I use to combine research and writing, and just get the bones of the work done. This is a process you can use when you're writing anything. Use it for your proposal, the book itself, writing advertising material – I even use it for writing copy for businesses and for novels. The best thing about this process is that it stops you from getting stuck.

1) Idea/ topic/ subject

2) Ten minutes of research

3) Word lists

4) Timed free-writing for five minutes

5) Take a break

6) First draft

1. *Idea/ topic/ subject*

If you've got an idea you want to develop, write it at the top of a sheet of paper.

In this instance, write the title you've chosen for your first chapter. I use colored pencils and paper for this part of the process so that I can doodle all around the page, but feel free to open a new document in your word processor if you want to type.

If you don't have a topic or a title for your chapter, just get a blank sheet of paper or open a new document, and keep following the steps of the process.

2. *Ten minutes of research*

This research process is really just an early-warning for your subconscious mind, to stimulate it and to get it to start coming up with material.

I tend to browse the Web for research whatever I happen to be working on, because I can always find something that starts me thinking. For example, one week I was ready to work on five radio spots for a jewellery store. I browsed online jewellery stores, and museum sites. Within five minutes I hit on an information nugget that stimulated a train of thought. Whatever topic you're writing on for your proposal, browse a few Web sites which are related.

3. *Word lists*

I love word lists. They take no effort at all, and they're ideal for kick-starting any kind of writing. I use them for fiction, for non-fiction and for copywriting. I also write them just for practice, to get my brain ticking over. Here's part of a word list I wrote this morning: "Glamor fear isolation energy deliver storm glow wind moon rush generosity travel stream voice density". You can see that on one level, it's just a laundry-list of words. On another level, what if I asked you to write half a page of a story, using these three words: "Fear Storm Generosity" somewhere in the first paragraph? You could do it, and you'd find it easy.

I could use this list to develop a scene for a chapter in a novel, or to develop a new character for the novel. But I'm currently working on an advertorial for digital imaging products for a computer magazine, so the word list gives me some ideas to play with for that. The list even gives me some ideas I could develop for magazine articles and essays. Not bad for fifteen words which took a few seconds to write.

For your book proposal, just start making lists of words. The idea is not to direct your thoughts at all, just list all the words which spring to mind. Don't limit yourself with words directly related to the subject of you proposal. You may never use your word lists in your work at all. I think of them as ways of prodding my subconscious. After I've filled half a page of words, I may or may not use them. I don't look on writing the lists as a waste of time, however, because writing them gets me into a creative mood.

4. *Timed free-writing for five minutes*

The topic for your free-writing session will be the title of your first chapter.

I'm a fan of free-writing. If you haven't read Peter Elbow's amazing books, particularly Writing With Power, get hold of the book as soon as you can. After reading it, I guarantee you you'll never have problems with getting words onto the page ever again.

Timed free-writing is just what it sounds like. You set a timer, and put pen to paper, or get your fingers traveling across the keyboard. At the end of the time you set, you stop writing. You don't have to write in complete sentences. You can write fragments of thoughts, or even write a word list. Just write whatever words appear in your mind. Don't put any pressure on yourself. Even if you have a report that needs to be finished in an hour, don't make the subject of your report the topic for your free-writing session. Let whatever words want to come out, emerge. You can whine onto the page about how hard writing is for five minutes, if you wish. If you do, you'll feel better for having released that limiting thought.

5. *Take a break*

Close your notebook, switch off your computer and leave your desk. Your break can be short, but take at least ten minutes. Preferably half an hour or an hour. I mean it --- LEAVE YOUR DESK.

6. *First draft*

When you return to your desk, don't look at any of your word lists, or your free-writing session. Just start to work on a first draft of your outline, and some material for your first chapter. Write as quickly as you can.

I do first drafts on the computer, and I try to type fast, just following whatever thoughts happen to strike me, and not paying any attention to typos or to format. If I'm writing an article or advertising copy, or anything which is under a thousand words, I write the first draft straight through. I aim to take an hour or less to do this. At this stage, my aim is just to get the words written. I can worry about whether they're the right words later. Right now, I just want words.

You will find that the words come quickly, and that you not only outline your first chapter, but several additional chapters.

What goes into your chapter outline?

You don't need to create the kind of outline that your English teacher harassed you into creating when you were 12. The kind of outline you need to create is one based on components. Non-fiction is much easier to write than fiction because all non-fiction books similar components. Let's have a look at some of them:

> (1) A foreword. This is similar to an introduction, but a foreword is usually written by someone other than the author of the book. It helps if you can get someone famous to contribute the foreword.
> Note: They may expect payment for this. If this person would lend great credibility to your book, then consider paying them for the foreword. It could make the

difference between whether your proposal is easy to sell, or more difficult. If you're writing in an area in which you don't have professional expertise --- for example, if you're writing about a medical topic and you're not a doctor --- then getting a foreword written by a professional is worthwhile.

(2) An introduction. This is optional. If you can't think of anything to put in an introduction, leave it out. Think of including an introduction if you want to tell your own story: how you came to get the information you're about to share.

(3) A "How To Use This book" chapter or page. This can be short, or quite long. For example, if you're writing a book on yoga, you could use this chapter to give four or five exercise routines, compiled from the various poses that you discuss in the rest of the book.

(4) Chapters with problems and solutions. For example, if you were writing a book on dieting, you could write seven chapters all posing a typical problem, and then provide solutions for each problem.

(5) The last chapter is the wrap-up. In this chapter you'll want to give readers instructions on where they go from here, and you'll also want to include an inspirational message.

(6) A glossary is useful if it will be necessary for readers new to the subject area. For example, if your book contains a lot of industry jargon with which your reader is unfamiliar, give explanations of terminology here.

(7) An index. I'm always disappointed when an otherwise excellent book, that I'll be referring to again, omits an index. I know creating an index is a hassle, but if you think your readers will use it, then go the extra mile and include it.

Will you need graphics or photographs?

If your book needs photos or other graphics, start thinking about them now. For example, if you're writing about petcare, then by all means send along a couple of relevant photos or graphics with your proposal. However, illustrative material is only useful if it adds value for the reader. Do the other books which cover the same subject as your book include graphics?

If you decide that your book must have graphics, mention this in your proposal. Send along an image or two, even if you've only taken them with your own digital camera.

Day Five: Write your proposal query letter, and submit it to agents and publishers

Day Five Tasks

Task One: Start a contact list of agents and publishers

Finding an agent/ publisher is the first step to selling your book proposal. However, even after you've sold your proposal, you'll want to stay current with agent and publisher news in order to sell your next proposal, and the one after that.

Start a contact list of agents and publishers, and as you find snippets of information online, or in your offline reading, enter notes into your database. Information you might want to add includes: recent sales and the amount the book was sold for, movements of editors from one publishing house to the next, and publishing house changes.

Collecting and maintaining all this information shouldn't be viewed as a chore. It's vital business intelligence. It could also help you to increase your income by many thousands of dollars each year.

Task Two: Send out ten query letters to agents and publishers

Agents and publishers take time to respond. So today you'll create a query letter for your proposal, and will send it out to ten agents and publishers. You can choose to send only to agents, or only to publishers, or you may want to send out five to each group.

Today you write your proposal query letter

Now you're written the blurb for your book, and the chapter outline, the next step is to start asking agents and publishers whether they're interested in looking at the proposal for your book. This means that you'll send out a query letter, asking agents and publishers to look at your proposal.

Note: some new authors want to omit this step. They figure --- hey, I'll just send the complete proposal, so I get a response faster. Unfortunately, sending a complete unsolicited proposal will SLOW the process. Agents and publishers receive so many packages of material that they stack them in a spare office, and the office junior gets to read them once every couple of months. Send a query letter, then send the proposals to those people who've asked to see it.

Do you need an agent?

Yes. And no. It can sometimes be harder to get an agent than it is to get a publisher, so it's a good idea to query both. When you get an agent, you can tell the agent which publishers you've already queried. If you get an agent before you get a publisher, you can approach agents who are a good fit for your book to ask them whether they will handle the contract negotiations for you.

You definitely need an agent if you intend to write more than one book. As to whether you should go agent-hunting, the answer is a definite yes. This isn't only because an agent will take a lot of the submission and negotiation workload, and because the agent has (one hopes) her fingers constantly on the pulse of publishing and knows what's going on, it's also because an agent forms a handy cut-off switch between you and the publisher. When problems occur --- let's say that your editor's demands annoy you, or that your advance payments are late, you've got someone to gripe at other than your editor.

On the other hand, if you'd rather keep all the profits your book makes, and feel that you can handle your contract negotiations yourself, you may want to skip agents, and focus on publishers.

Online resources to help you in your agent-hunt

Here's a list of online resources which will help you to decide whether or not you want an agent, and agent contact details.

WritersNet: http://www.writers.net/agents/browse/loc.php

This is an excellent site, with many useful articles telling you what agents do, as well as agent lists you can browse.

Literaryagents.org: http://www.literaryagents.org/

Another excellent site with articles and agent listings.

Index of US Literary Agents:
http://www.writersservices.com/WrHandbook/wh_us_index.htm

This page is on the Writer's Services site, and you'll also find listings of UK agents.

Preditors and Editors: http://www.anotherealm.com/prededitors/

You'll want to bookmark this site. It's a wonderful resource to help you to maintain your writing career.

Literary Agent Warnings: http://www.sfwa.org/beware/agents.html

Unfortunately, as in all fields, in writing there are scam artists. This page, maintained by the Science Fiction and Fantasy Writers of America Inc, gives you the low-down (pun intended) on literary scammers.

Note: things change fast online. Do your own "literary agents" query on www.Google.com and other search engines for additional agent information and listings.

Sending your query letter directly to publishers

Many large publishers will not look at unagented material. However, this still leaves many who will. And most will look at any letter that you care to send them. Because a publisher can buy your book, and because you're likely to get a much faster response from a publisher than you will from an agent, I recommend that in addition to sending out your queries to agents, you also send them to publishers.

The best resource for finding publisher information online is Writersmarket.com at http://www.writersmarket.com

From the Web site:

>>

WritersMarket.com is your wired key to publishing success, providing the most comprehensive—and always up-to-date—market contact info available, with electronic tools you won't find anywhere else. And it's all risk-free. Sign up today and get:

- ✓ More markets than you'll find anywhere else. And with our constantly updated and verified contact listings, you'll find the market information you need to get your work into the hands of the right editor or agent today.

- ✓ Easy-to-use searches. Looking for a specific magazine or book publisher? Just type in the title. Or, widen your prospects with our new keyword search for broad category results.

- ✓ Expert advice from top editors, agents and writers. Want to know how to improve your cover and query letters? Have a question for an editor or agent? Find the answer you need here.

✓ Daily industry updates. Debbi Ridpath Ohi has her finger on the publishing pulse - and she shares her insider info with you.

✓ Plus, personalize your home page, keep track of your work with Submission Tracker, save your best prospects in Favorites' Folders, and more!

>> Please note, I don't have any connection to Writersmarket.com, aside from subscribing to the service. I've been a subscriber for several years, and have always been happy with the service. It will save you a lot of time looking for publishers. Of course, the service isn't restricted to publisher listings. You'll find agent listings as well, plus magazine listings and a library of useful articles.

Yes, you can multiple-submit your query letter, and even your proposal

Once you start marketing your proposal, you'll find that some agents and publishers include words like "no multiple submissions" when they're telling authors how they want to receive proposals. In other words, they want exclusivity. Unfortunately, there's a big problem with this. The problem is time. Most agents and editors will take a month or longer to evaluate your proposal. Some take as long as six months. Considering that you may need to approach 20 to 30 editors and/ or publishers, you could still be sending out your book three years from now. Professional writers ignore these admonitions, because if they didn't, they wouldn't eat.

Sample Query Letter

What goes into a query letter? I've included a sample query letter that I've sent out, and which garnered an agent contract immediately. You'll see that this letter is:

- Short;
- To the point.

I could have spent a lot longer composing this letter --- I could have included a better hook, and included the book's blurb. At the time I sent it out however, I didn't have the time to spend on revisions. I'm including this plain-vanilla, so-so query letter here for a reason. That is --- and I've found this to be true in 25 years of writing --- it's important that you SHOW UP. In other words, while you might want each piece of writing you send out to be perfect, or at least brilliant, sometimes you don't have the time. At those times, send it out anyway.

Get into the habit of treating your work with a certain amount of aplomb. That is, even thought it's not perfect, and you could make it better if you had the time and energy, 90 per cent of the time what matters is that you send out your work. If you're a closet perfectionist, as I am, this will be hard for you at first.

XXX

XXX

[DATE]

Dear XX

My name is Beau Tighe. I'm seeking representation for my book: [Title Excerpted].

The book is aimed at writers who would like to make money by copywriting (writing for business). As a copywriter, writers write the words that sell: everyday words. The words on ads, leaflets, brochures, press releases, product instructions and labels, newsletters, direct mail, and on Web sites.

I've been selling the material as an ebook and as an e-course on my Web site (http://yourwebsitehere.com/) for several months. It has been well received, and now I'd like to take the material and use it as the basis for a book.

Although there are several popular books on copywriting, none approach the material in a step-by-step fashion. My book's constructed so that at the end of seven days and seven lessons, the reader has built a viable freelance copywriting business.

My credentials for writing the book: I've been both a successful copywriter and writer for over 25 years. I've included a brief bio below.

Please let me know if you'd like to see a proposal for the book.

Sincerely

Beau Tighe

Bio:

Australian author and journalist Beau Tighe writes about business, technology, women's issues, and creativity. Her books include: [Title Excerpted], [Title Excerpted], I[Title Excerpted], and [Title Excerpted]. Her feature articles have appeared in [Title Excerpted], [Title Excerpted], [Title Excerpted], [Title Excerpted], and numerous other print and online magazines.

~~Beau Tighe partial list of credits~~

A professional writer for 25 years, her credits include:

* [Credit Excerpted]

* [Credit Excerpted]

* [Credit Excerpted]

* [Credit Excerpted]

* [Credit Excerpted]

At her Web site (http://yourwebsitehere.com/), Beau Tighe publishers three popular ezines: [Title Excerpted] and [Title Excerpted], which are free to subscribers, and [Title Excerpted], which has paying subscribers. She also teaches online writing courses.

Another sample query letter

Here's another sample query letter. At the time of writing, I haven't sent out this letter. Again however, you can see that it's short, to the point, and contains nothing irrelevant. Over the years, I've found that whether I'm pitching (selling) nonfiction or fiction, I've had the best responses to letters which were less than one page in length.

Remember that nothing is set in stone. It's all an experiment. Write your letter at whatever length seems best to you. Your motto should be: "whatever works".

XXXX

XXXX

[DATE]

Dear XX

My name is Beau Tighe. I'm seeking representation for my book: [Title Excerpted]. The target audience is writers, and aspiring writers, who want to be paid for their skill with words.

[Title Excerpted] discusses the new earning power that Internet technology gives writers. Many writers are comfortable using the Internet for email and research, but most are unaware that they now have many new opportunities, including:

- Clever new ways to market their work and services with tools like autoresponders, email mini-courses, ebooks, and promotional ezines;

- The opportunity to develop a loyal following of readers. They can write and publish instantly, to a worldwide audience millions strong, with tools like Web logs (blogs);

- The ability to target specific niches, and to garner an income much faster than they can via traditional publishing routes. A writer can write an ebook or report this month, and sell it forever.

I've been selling this material as an ebook and as an e-course on my Web site (http://yourwebsitehere.com/) for several months. It has been well received, and now I'd like to take the material and use it as the basis for a book.

My credentials for writing the book: I've been an author, writer and copywriter over 25 years. I've been online since 1993, and know the online world well. (I've included a brief bio below.)

As far as I'm aware, there's no other book currently on the market which presents this material. The few Internet-related books for writers currently available came out around 2000, during the height of the dot com boom, and focus on online markets for writers.

Please let me know if you'd like to see a proposal for the book.

Sincerely

Beau Tighe

Write your query letter!

The next step is to write your own query letter. Don't take too long over this. Make a couple of notes of points you want to include, and write it. You can include your blurb --- your blurb could in fact make up the bulk of your letter.

Here's a quick outline for your letter:

A. Introduce yourself in 20 words or less, and state your business --- "I'm seeking representation for my book: [title]..."

B. Blurb.

C. Your credentials.

D. Identify the market for the book.

"Don'ts" for your query letter

1. Don't make unsupported claims for yourself or your book

Please don't say that you're successful or that you've written a bestseller. Only beginning writers make claims like this. The agent or editor will immediately classify you as a novice, and an irritating one at that.

(On the other hand, if a well-known much-published writer has praised you or your book, say so, and give his/ her contact details so that the editor can call him/ her.)

2. Don't mention that you're unpublished

The agent will figure it out when you don't mention writing credits. Please note: THIS IS NOT A BAD THING. Everyone has to start somewhere. Editors and agents know this, and they won't hold it against you. They will judge your book proposal query on its merits. If an agent feels that your material is something that she can sell, she will contact you. As will an editor, if she feels that the writing in your query letter is to the point and professional, and she thinks that your book idea is a good one.

3. Don't mention that your partner, your best friend, or the milkman think that you're a good writer or that you've got a brilliant idea for a book

Unless these people have publishing credits, no one cares. Mentioning them marks you not only as an amateur, but also as someone who may be difficult to work with.

What do I mean by "difficult to work with"? Before you sign a contract, your agent and editor will judge your behaviour, looking for tell-tale signs that you might be a problem writer.

Problem writers:

- Argue when asked to rewrite. Almost everything you write will need to be rewritten. Your agent will ask you to add, delete or revise material in your proposal. Your editor will ask for rewrites on your book, and perhaps more than one rewrite. Therefore, if you show any sign that you may drag your feet over these chores, or do them without a song on your lips, they will dump you. Life's too short, and publishing is too competitive to indulge anyone's temperament;

- Procrastinate. Publishing is always on a tight deadline. From the day of your first contact, you must show that you can work to deadline.

- Can't follow instructions. Never be afraid to ask if there is something you don't understand. For example, if you're asked for a "bio" and you don't know how to write one, ask. No one will think less of you for asking, but they will take several steps backward if you don't follow instructions, or if you decide that you will do things your way.

- Turn in a messy or less-than-pristine typescript. Or fail to send an electronic file when asked.

4. Don't be specific

Many writers are never asked for a proposal because they don't nail the query letter. If you tell an agent your book is about "growing up in the fifties", the agent will simply ignore you. This is not specific enough. You must be totally specific, so that the person you're writing to can visualise the book, and can also visualise where it will fit into the marketplace.

Writers do this sort of thing because they're insecure. They imagine that if they're vague, the agent will ask to see their book because they want to know exactly what it's about. This is a HUGE mistake. Agents and editors receive hundreds of letters and proposals each week. If you're not specific, you give the impression that you haven't thought out your proposal.

Day Six: Write the proposal

Day Six Task

Task One: Write the initial draft of your book proposal

Write the draft quickly. Don't think too much about it. In your initial draft, you aim for quantity, rather than quality.

Relax! You'll write your draft in stages

Today's the big day. You're going to write your book proposal. If you're starting to freeze up at the thought, relax. You've already done a lot of preparation work, and you're not going to write it all at once. You'll write it by taking the proposal through several clearly defined stages:

A. First draft. This is your "thinking" draft, in which you think on paper. In this draft, you write whatever you like. You're aiming for quantity here, rather than quality. Write this draft full-steam ahead, without stopping to look things up. Consider "writing" this draft by talking into a tape recorder.

If you need to do some spot research, just leave a note to yourself, and keep working on the draft. You can look up individual items later. The benefit of doing specific research later is that you may find it's unnecessary. It's quite possible that you'll eliminate this material from a later draft.

B. Your second draft. Your first draft has shown you what you want to say. In this draft, you have a crack at saying it. In your second draft, you organize. You decide what material you want to include, and perhaps expand on, and what material you'll delete. Think of this draft as shaping your material.

Occasionally you'll want to take this shaping draft through several documents. You may have a B1, B2, B3 and B4 version, for example.

Keep your drafts.

Use the "File, Save As" menu option of your word processor to keep versions of your book proposal. When you change the name of the file as you work through different versions, it means that you can always go back and reinsert something that you deleted, because it's in a previous version.

C. Your clean-up draft. Your final draft. You've said what you want to say, now you get a chance to say it better. You clean up the redundancies and spice it up.

Paradoxically, the easiest way to write well is to allow yourself to write badly. Every day. This is because writing is hard when you try to think and write at the same time. Allow yourself to think on paper for as many drafts as you need. Then write the final draft with confidence.

Woody Allen once said that 90 per cent of success at anything was just showing up. I've found that that's very true. So no matter how bad you feel your writing is at any given time, go ahead anyway. Your writing is not as bad as you think, it's simply a crisis of confidence, and even if it is rough when you first get it on the computer screen, it can be fixed. However, if you hesitate, and don't get it on the computer screen, you have nothing to fix. Get it done!

At the end of this book, in the Appendix, you'll find the complete proposal for my book [Title Excerpted]. This is a real proposal, and it won an agent contract on first reading. Read it through so that you can see exactly what goes into creating a proposal.

We've already covered what your proposal must contain, here it is again, for reference. Please print this page out:

- A title page, with the title, subtitle, author, word count of the completed book, and estimated time frame for completion. You might state: "75,000 words, completion three months after agreement".

- An overview: a description of the book. This can be as short as a paragraph, or several pages long.

- The background of the author. Your biography, as it relates to your expertise for this book.

- The competition in the marketplace. This is where you mention the top four or five titles which are your book's competitors. (Note: if there are dozens of competitors for your book, this is a good thing, because it means that the subject area is popular. Your book will need to take a new slant.)

- Promotions. This is where you describe how you will promote your book, both before and after publication.

- A chapter outline.

- A sample chapter, or two chapters. This is always the first chapter, and if you're sending two chapters, it's the Introduction and Chapter One, or if there's no Introduction, it's Chapters One and Two.

- Attachments. Optional. You may want to attach articles you've written about the book's topic, or any relevant supporting material.

Let's write the proposal

Your chapter outline

You've already been working on a major part of the proposal --- the chapter outline. If you like, you can begin today's work by spending an hour or two with that. If your chapter outline still has major holes in it, don't worry too much about it. Today we'll complete an initial draft of the complete proposal, and you can fill in the gaps later.

Your background—why you're the person to write this book

Next, we'll work on the background section.

The first piece of info you'll need to include in the background section is a brief bio. Every book you own has a bio of the author, so take a few books off your shelves and study the author bios. Most are short. Novelists' bios mention the writer's interests, partner, children and pets. The bios of nonfiction writers (that's you) emphasize the writer's academic credentials if it's important to the writer's credibility, or the writer's experience in the field the book covers, or anything else which might be relevant.

Here's an example of a bio, which I wrote as part of the book proposal for: [Title Excerpted]

Quick Bio

A professional writer for 25 years, her credits include:

* [Credit Excerpted]

* [Credit Excerpted]

* [Credit Excerpted]

* [Credit Excerpted]

* [Credit Excerpted]

At her Web site (http://yourwebsitehere.com/), Beau Tighe publishers three popular ezines: [Title Excerpted] and [Title Excerpted], which are free to subscribers, and [Title Excerpted], which has paying subscribers. She also teaches online writing courses.

Your bio must be slanted so that it relates to those experiences which make you the perfect person to write the book you're proposing. For example, let's say that in your daily life you're a doctor. The book you're proposing is a gardening book: how to grow your own organic vegetables. In your bio, might call yourself "Dr. Jane Smith", but for this bio, you'd mention that you grew up on a farm, have grown organic vegetables for ten years, and write a monthly column for Eat Your Organic Veggies Magazine. Your experiences as a doctor wouldn't be appropriate for this book. On the other hand (just to confuse you), if you intended to cover the health and nutritional benefits of organic vegetables at great length, then your credentials as a doctor would be important, and you'd include them.

Please remember that there is no way you can do any of this wrong --- something either works, or it doesn't. You can always make changes later, when you get feedback .

Many of my writing students focus so much on the "correct" way of doing something, that they never get anything done. Join any writing group, and discussions of correct formatting abound. If you start to get nervous about anything you're doing, wondering whether you're doing it "right", simply tell yourself: "this is the way I choose to do it. I may choose another way at some other time, but right now, I do it this way, and it's the right way for me."

In addition to your bio, if you have publishing credits you'll want to mention them here. Your publishing credits should be paid credits, rather than work you've done for promotional purposes, or material for which you weren't paid.

What if you don't have any publishing credits? Everyone has to start somewhere. If you don't have any credits, don't worry about them. If your proposal is excellent, and a publisher wants to commission the book, then your lack of credits won't count against you.

Write the Overview

Now you'll know why you spent time writing your blurb. The Overview, the description of your book, is the first part of your proposal that agents and publishers will read. It's your book in a nutshell. It's also merely an expanded version of your blurb.

I've included a sample Overview below. It's from the proposal for my book Writing To Sell In The Internet Age.

Sample Overview [Title Excerpted]

The Internet gives writers unlimited new opportunities

[Title Excerpted] empowers writers by revealing the immense new earning power that Internet technology gives them. While many writers are comfortable using the Internet for email and research, most are unaware that they now have many new opportunities, including:

- Clever new ways to market their work and services with tools like autoresponders, email mini-courses, ebooks, auctions, and promotional ezines;

- The opportunity to develop a loyal following of readers. They can write and publish instantly, to a worldwide audience millions strong, with tools like Web logs (blogs). This loyal following makes a writer more appealing to traditional publishers;

- The ability to target specific niches, and to garner an income much more quickly than they can via traditional publishing routes. A writer can write an ebook or report this month, and sell it forever.

The Internet gives writers the power to be their own publisher and distributor by selling their work directly to readers. Many writers are already taking advantage of the possibilities. Judy Cullins, who's building an online reputation as "The Book Coach", says of selling her ebooks online directly to readers: "The first months, I had no idea at the time how powerful this method was. My income bolted to over $3000 a month in less than a year."

The new rule for writers in the Internet age is: "Create, promote, sell". What's amazing is that writers can do all this in one day, even in hours. When I write a report, I can format it in PDF (Portable

Document Format) at the click of a key. That's the publishing done. I can then add the report to the online store at my Web site in minutes --- distribution done. Then I can send an announcement out to my subscribers (promotion done) and watch the sales rolling in. Best of all I don't have to be anywhere in particular to do this. I can do it as easily on a sun-drenched beach on the Great Barrier Reef off northern Australia as I can in my home office in Sydney.

Are these capabilities within the reach of non-technically-inclined writers? Yes! Although I've been writing about software, computers and the Internet for many years, I'm by no means a geek. The writers who shared their anecdotes and success stories for this book aren't geeks either. They're writers who've seen opportunities and grabbed at them. Many of these writer/ publisher/ entrepreneurs didn't come to writing via traditional publishing routes. Many started out as marketers, or entrepreneurs. They looked at the Internet, saw how relatively easy it is to make money selling information online, and worked out ways to do it. The Internet is the answer to writers' prayers. It puts writers in control of their own destinies.

We see what we expect to see, so writers have seen the Internet as a magazine-style "content" market. But because of the unlimited free content online, few sites buy content. (This may change, as more sites with good content change to a reader-pays business model.) Writers haven't yet seen that the Internet is a completely new environment, where they can write what they want to write, and can, without too much effort, make a good living.

A how-to plus a how-they-did-it

[Title Excerpted] is a how-to for writers to access their new opportunities, but it's also a how-they-did-it. I'll be describing the avenues that writer-entrepreneurs are developing to use the Internet to make excellent money in many new ways. These writers are exploring their new options with amazement and delight. It's an exciting time. I'll be including their stories and tips in this book to inspire other writers that they can do it too.

What I won't be including

I won't include descriptions of technology and the online environment. Information on how to build a Web site, how to sell online, how to create a mailing list and other technical minutiae is readily available online. Also because technology is advancing so quickly, technical information rapidly becomes outdated. What won't change however are the basic concepts of writing to sell in the Internet age.

Include in your Overview:

➤ A description of your book;

➤ Why your book is important;

➤ Something about what's included in your book;

➤ Why you're the person to write this book.

Don't hype, BUT DO INCLUDE EVERYTHING RELEVANT

Please don't try to hype your book in the Overview. Just tell your story as quickly and as clearly as you can.

Also, don't hold anything back. I've read many proposals from beginning writers where the writer has tried to be coy: "For the complete details, you'll need to read the book!" This kind of thing will work against you. You're asking a publisher to invest around $30,000 to publish your book. Anyone who's going to spend that amount of money wants all the details. Please provide them.

Your Overview's length

Your Overview can be as long, or as short, as you feel it needs to be. Some proposals have one-page Overviews, in others, the writer needs five pages to describe the book. Use your own judgement here. If you need five pages, then by all means, use them. However, if your Overview is long, make sure that you haven't repeated information.

Write the Promotions section

Next, you'll write the Promotions section. In this section, you will show your publisher that you intend to go all-out to promote your book. You can do this with an investment of money, or of time. If you can do both, you should.

Promoting with money

Company CEOs, sports figures, celebrities and other well-heeled people often write books, or have books written for them by ghost-writers. It's understood that any celebrity will hire a public relations agency, and will spend a lot of money nudging the book up the bestseller list. If you have money to spend on a public relations agency, mention this in your proposal. Your publisher will be pleased that you intend to get behind the book.

Promoting with time

If you don't have swags of cash lying around that you can use to promote your book, you'll need to invest time. There are a million ways you can promote your book, from pasting magnetic letters onto your car and building a Web site to calling bookstores all over the country to talk them into stocking your book. You can even act as your own PR agency, and without anything other than an Internet connection and some time, can do a lot of work to help sell your book. Anything that you do will be appreciated by the publisher.

Sample Promotions section [Title Excerpted]

Here's the Promotions section from [Title Excerpted]:

My primary focus will be on online promotions. For two reasons: I'm located in Australia, which means I can't go the usual book store/ speaking venue route to promote the book. And I've been online since 1992, pre-World Wide Web, and know how to promote online. (I wrote a book called [Title Excerpted], which is about setting up a small business online (1998, [publisher])). Also, it's appropriate to promote a book about selling in the age of the Internet on the Internet.

I have a popular Web site (http://yoursitegoeshere.com/) and three email ezines, and I'll be promoting [Title Excerpted] heavily in all of them. Each of these posts are also promoted on Facebook and Twitter, as well as other social media networks. I now spend ten hours a week working on my site and my ezines, and on promotional activities for them, so I'll increase that to 15 hours, so that I regularly spend considerable time on the book's promotion.

My offline focus will be on getting press coverage and radio interviews.

My plan outline

- ✔ I will create a mini-Web site for [Title Excerpted] . This will be a three page sales site, the name of the site to be taken from the book. Such mini-sites are called "buy, bookmark or leave" sites. The entire site is similar to a direct mail letter: its only purpose is to encourage the reader to buy the book. The beauty of such sites is that if they're efficiently linked from other sites, such as my business site, [Title Excerpted], and other sites in which I have an interest, they quickly rank #1 in the search top search engines, that is, in Yahoo! and Google.com.

✔ I'll write a long sales page on my website for [Title Excerpted]. (See an example: http://yourwebsitehere.com/sample-page.html)

✔ I'll develop an email newsletter for the book's buyers, and prospective buyers. This monthly newsletter will update the information in the book, and will include a link for readers to buy the book online.

✔ I'll subscribe to a press release Web site, so I can send out monthly online news releases for the book to thousands of media outlets in the U.S., and if the book gets a Commonwealth sale, in the UK and Australia. With the phone, email and fax, doing long-distance interviews for newspapers and radio will be easy. Several of my books have attracted radio and newspaper interviews, and I'm comfortable doing them.

✔ I'll interact in online chat rooms, conferences, and in mailing lists, subtly promoting the book.

✔ I'll create a private discussion group for the book's readers in the "Talk" forums section of my [Title Excerpted] Web site, so that readers can ask questions and interact with me directly. As this forum grows, I'll appoint reader-moderators for the various discussions.

Write the Competition section

On Day Two, you did a lot of work on assessing the market for your book. Here's where you use all that information. Choose anywhere from three to five books which you estimate will be your book's main competitors. Describe how your book is different from these books, and how your book fills a niche in the marketplace.

Include the names of the books, the authors, and the year of publication. If these books were published several years ago, this is all to the good.

Day Seven: Write the sample chapter and revise your proposal

Day Seven Tasks

Task One: Write the sample chapter

Write the first chapter of your book.

Task Two: Revision

Revise the first draft of your complete proposal.

Today you write your sample chapter

Write your sample chapter using the A,B, and C method that we talked about. I've also described a fast method that I use to write chapters of books below. If you prefer to use a tape recorder, then by all means do that. I prefer to write first drafts by hand, on yellow legal pads. I find that I can relax and enjoy myself when I write by hand. Whichever method you use, just settle down and write the first chapter.

Note: invariably, after you sell the proposal, and are writing the book, you will make changes and it's likely that the final first chapter you write will be very different from the version you're writing today. Since that's the case, just write as quickly as you can.

A fast chapter-writing method

Writing a chapter of a book is like writing a long article. Most chapters are somewhere between 2000 and 4000 words, but if you want to write a short chapter of 1500 words, that's fine too. Remember that you can't do any of this wrong, and it's your choice.

Here's a method that I use when I'm writing a chapter in a book. Adapt it to your own needs.

1. Reread your notes

Reread the notes that you've made during this week.

2. Talk to yourself on paper

Then take five minutes and write out exactly what you want to include in this chapter. This isn't an outline; your notes can be as brief, or as lengthy as you wish. I usually talk to myself on paper, like this:

"What do I want to cover in this chapter? I want the reader to understand (this process/ theory/ idea/ method). I also want to include these five anecdotes. What do the anecdotes show? The first one shows that..."

By talking to myself like this, I eliminate performance anxiety. Some writers do the same thing by writing their chapters as letters: they can take it easy, as if they're talking to a friend. The big benefit of using a method like this is that it does away with formality and stiffness.

3. When you're ready, write

When you feel ready, start to write. As you're writing, just get the words out as quickly as you can. It's useful to set a goal for the number of pages in an hour. I usually aim for three pages an hour. However, if you feel that having a number of pages that you "must" write an hour stresses you, then don't set a goal like this.

When you're writing:

- ✔ Turn on the answering machine, and turn off your email program;

- ✔ Close your office door;

- ✔ Set yourself goal of either pages written, or words written;

- ✔ Don't reread your notes. If you need to look something up, just write "tk" which is an old printer's mark meaning "to come", and keep on writing. If you stop to look something up it may derail your train of thought. Plus you may think: oh, I need to cover this, and this, and this must go in. Assure yourself that you won't be able to cover everything. Trust that your subconscious will deliver the material which needs to go into the first chapter ;

- ✔ Keep going even if you're sure that what you're writing is less than your best work. You can tidy it all up later. Just get the words down.

If you find that your writing goes slowly with this first chapter, that's normal. First chapters are always slow to write, because you haven't found the right tone and voice in which to write your book. Once you find those, the writing will go much more easily. Because first chapters are always slow, it's important that you don't leave your desk until you've written the number of words you set out to write.

Revising your proposal

When you've completed the first chapter, print out the entire proposal. Then go and do something else --- go and watch a movie, or have lunch. Take a good break of at least a couple of hours before you come back to read your proposal.

How to revise

Just like your writing, your revision will go through several phases. Copyediting, or line revision, where you fiddle with word choices and grammar, comes last.

Here are the steps:

1. Read the entire proposal

Read the proposal straight through. Keep note-making to a minimum. This is so you can get a sense of how the material reads. When you've finished this initial read-through, ask yourself whether what you've written stays close to your blurb. If it doesn't, you can either change your blurb --- perhaps you've been inspired with some creative new ideas --- or you can change your proposal.

While this read-through is fresh in your mind, write out your impressions. Have you covered most of what you want to include? What else do you think the proposal needs?

2. Slash and burn

Before you start cutting, rename your document (Version B or B1, or whatever naming process makes sense to you).

Now go through the proposal and take out the material that you've decided you want to eliminate. If it's too painful to simply hit the Delete key, cut the material and paste it into another document.

3. Add material

In this pass through the proposal, add the material the proposal needs. Perhaps you've done some additional research --- write up all the material you want to include.

4. Read for coherency

Print out your proposal, and read it through to check for coherency. Make sure that you've included transitions in your sample chapter.

5. Revise for style

In this pass through the material, you get to jazz it up, if you wish.

6. Copyedit

In this final pass through your proposal, check for grammar and word usage.

You're done!

You've done it, congratulations!

You've completed your book proposal. Now comes the fun part, selling your proposal. If you need any help with this, you can contact me at any time. Don't forget to send me a copy of the ms for your free appraisal.

Good luck. See you on the bestseller lists. :-)

Appendix: Sample Book Proposal

[Title Excerpted]

by Beau Tighe

Proposal

- Words: 60,000
- Complete ms: three months.

Beau Tighe

E-mail: beatighe@gmail.com

World Wide Web: http://yourwebsitehere.com/

Overview

[Title Excerpted] shows writers how to set up their own copywriting services business in seven days. Its target market is writers, professional or aspiring, who want to make money from their writing skills. Melanie Rigney, editor of Writer's Digest magazine, estimated that ten per cent of the US population aspire to write.

From the book's Introduction:

Want to make REAL money writing?

You know you can write. Maybe you're even making money writing. But are you making enough money writing? Or is it just a hobby, costing you more in computers, postage and paper than you're earning? According to writers' organizations, 95 per cent of writers never make enough money to quit their day job.

What about the top five per cent of writers --- they're making big money, right? A small proportion of the top five per cent sure are. They're the headliners --- brand name writers like Stephen King and Dean Koontz. Journeymen (and women) writers are doing OK too. They're the genre writers, writing romance, mystery and suspense, and non-fiction. Writers in this group spend a lot of time looking over their shoulder. Will their publisher accept their next book? Are they writing enough? (Gotta turn in at least two books this year.) What nasty reviews of their latest book will they find on Amazon.com today? Magazine writers may do well too if they combine magazine writing with writing books.

If you want to make real money from your writing skills, you can. And you can do it easily and quickly, in seven days. How? Start a copywriting services business.

I've been making good money as a copywriter for over 25 years. It's fun, creative and lucrative.

The business writing market is invisible to most writers

Most writers are aren't skilled at business, and don't know how business works. They're unaware that businesses hire writers, so they pitch their work to overcrowded markets. Copywriters (business writers) write to meet the communications needs of large and small businesses. The material they write includes marketing communications, proposals, public relations material, and Web site content.

If copywriting does register as a potential market, writers don't have any easy, practical guides to help them to access this market. While bookshop shelves are packed with how-to guides to writing novels and magazine articles, the small number of available copywriting books are dry and dull, and make copywriting sound about as much fun as doing your own dentistry.

[Title Excerpted] aims to correct this. It's aimed at both professional and new writers. At the end of seven days, the enthusiastic new copywriter will have all the information and experience she needs to set up her own copywriting services business and make money.

Does the material work? Yes! I've been teaching this material in online and offline classes, and selling it online as an ebook. I'll be including many exercises and samples: sample exercises written by my students, sample ads, sample press releases, templates, and check lists. And because the material is based on my own 25 years of copywriting experience, I'll be including lots of anecdotes and insider information.

Writers need this book

True to its "easy money" title, the book focuses on teaching the reader how to get copywriting work, not just on copywriting techniques. As far as I can tell, none of the other copywriting books currently available teach copywriters how to prospect for new business. And yet, going by my experience with students and my monitoring of writers' groups online, this information is what writers need most.

Other copywriting books just don't provide the nitty-gritty of self-promotion and marketing. Writers need details and encouragement to market themselves and their services, so I'll be making this book as forceful and motivating (and fun) as I can. One of my students said that she until she did one of my free sample courses, she wasn't aware that copywriting was something she could do. Now she knows that it is.

That's the takeaway I want to give readers: you can make money, easily, from your writing skills, and you can make it very quickly, no long apprenticeship needed.

The book's structure

Readers will find it easy to work with this book. It's set up in the form of days and weeks, with tasks and exercises for each chapter. As the reader does the exercises for each day, she's doing the work involved in setting up her own copywriting services business. No wasted time – she's working on developing her own small business from the very first day!

Each chapter contains:

1. Samples, written by my students, so that readers feel more comfortable with the work.

2. Copywriting techniques for the reader to refer to as she begins to work as a copywriter.

3. Exercises. The reader will use the exercises to build her copywriters' portfolio.

What's not in the book

I've left out material which is widely available elsewhere, such as:

4. How to set up a home business; and

5. Small business technology.

Beau Tighe's Background

Bio:

Australian author and journalist Beau Tighe writes about business, technology, women's issues, and creativity. Her books include: [Title Excerpted], [Title Excerpted], [Title Excerpted], and [Title Excerpted]. Her feature articles have appeared in [Title Excerpted], [Title Excerpted], [Title Excerpted], [Title Excerpted], and numerous other print and online magazines.

Beau Tighe partial list of credits

A professional writer for 25 years, her credits include:

* [Credit Excerpted]

* [Credit Excerpted]

* [Credit Excerpted]

* [Credit Excerpted]

* [Credit Excerpted]

At her Web site (http://yourwebsitegoeshere.com/), Beau Tighe publishers three popular ezines: [Title Excerpted] and [Title Excerpted], which are free to subscribers, and [Title Excerpted], which has paying subscribers. She also teaches online writing courses.

Why this author for this book?

Beau Tighe is a writer, a business person and a teacher. She knows copywriting both from the writer's and business owner's points of view, and because she teaches writing, she knows how to pass her skills on to others.

She has written professionally for most of her adult life; everything from romance novels to computer manuals. She understands how writers work and think. She has also managed several successful small businesses. She first developed her copywriting skills when she managed a dog training and boarding business, and found advertising so expensive that it was vital that each ad pulled, and pulled well.

Her love of writing and fascination with the creative process also led her to teach popular writing courses at community colleges, and now online. The material in [Title Excerpted] has been tested by her students, and it works.

Competition

The following three books are [Title Excerpted]'s competition.

1. The Elements of Copywriting: The Essential Guide to Creating Copy That Gets the Results You Want

by Gary Blake, Robert W. Bly

Publisher: Longman; 1st edition (September 1, 1998)

ISBN: 0028626303

This is a good general reference to copywriting techniques. It's aimed at small business or marketing people who want a simple copywriting guide. It's not directed at the same market (writers) as [Title Excerpted], and provides no instruction on how to set up a copywriting services business.

2. Teach Yourself Copywriting

by J. Jonathan Gabay

Publisher: McGraw-Hill/Contemporary Books; 2nd edition (January 31, 2001)

ISBN: 0658012010

Another general reference to copywriting techniques, aimed at business and marketing people. Again, it's not aimed at writers, nor does it help in setting up in business as a copywriter.

3. The Well-Fed Writer: Financial Self-Sufficiency As a Freelance Writer in Six Months or Less

by Peter Bowerman

Publisher: Fanove Publishing; (September 2000)

ISBN: 0967059844

This book comes closest to targeting the same market as [Title Excerpted]

Peter Bowerman has written a useful book. His background as a marketing executive gives him a strong sales emphasis. However, because he has a sales and marketing background, and not a background as a writer, he doesn't cover the marketing of a copywriting services business. (He calls copywriting freelance commercial writing.)

His experience with marketing make marketing processes self-evident to him, and he tends to gloss over them. However, marketing doesn't come naturally to many writers, as I've seen with my students. They struggle with marketing, and need instruction in basic marketing processes and concepts.

Who will buy [Title Excerpted] and why?

The strongest target group likely to buy this book is writers, whether employed or freelance, who want to diversify, and develop another income stream. Aspiring writers are also likely to buy it, seeing it as an opportunity to earn while they learn and develop their writing skills.

Additional target groups include:

- ☎ ⌷⌷ colleges which teach writing courses;

- ☎ ⌷⌷ people laid off from corporate marketing jobs – they will already have an awareness of the work done by copywriters; and

- ☎ ⌷⌷ early retirees, who want to develop an income, but don't want or need full employment.

My promotions plan for [Title Excerpted].

My primary focus will be on online promotions. For two reasons: I'm located in Australia, which means I can't go the usual book store/ speaking venue route to promote the book. I also have a greater depth of experience in the online world. I've been online since 1993, pre-World Wide Web, and know how to promote online. (I wrote a book called [Title Excerpted], which is about setting up a small business online (1998, publisher)).

I have a popular Web site (http://yourwebsitehere.com/) and three email ezines, and I'll be promoting [Title Excerpted] heavily in all of them. I now spend ten hours a week working on my site and my ezines, and on promotional activities for them, so I'll increase that to 15 hours, so that I regularly spend considerable time on the book's promotion.

My plan outline

- ✔ I will create a mini-Web site for [Title Excerpted]. This will be a three page sales site, the name of the site to be taken from the book. Such mini-sites are called "buy, bookmark or leave" sites. The entire site is similar to a direct mail letter: its only purpose is to encourage the reader to buy the book. The beauty of such sites is that if they're efficiently linked from other sites, such as my business site, [Title Excerpted], and other sites in which I have an interest, they quickly rank #1 in the search top search engines, that is, in Yahoo! and Google.com.

- ✔ I'll write a long sales page on [Title Excerpted] for [Title Excerpted]. (See an example: http://yourwebsitehere.com/ecourses2.html)

- ✔ I'll develop an email newsletter for the book's buyers, and prospective buyers. This monthly newsletter will update the information in the book, and will include a link for readers to buy the book online.

- ✔ I'll subscribe to a press release Web site, so I can send out monthly online news releases for the book to thousands of media outlets in the U.S., and if the book gets a Commonwealth sale, in the UK and Australia. With the phone, email and fax, doing long-distance interviews for newspapers and radio will be easy. Several of my books have attracted radio and newspaper interviews, and I'm comfortable doing them.

- ✔ I'll interact in online chat rooms, conferences, and in mailing lists, subtly promoting the book.

- ✔ I'll create a private discussion group for the book's readers in the "Talk" forums section of my [Title Excerpted] Web site, so that readers can ask questions and interact with me directly. As this forum grows, I'll appoint reader-moderators for the various discussions.

Chapter Outline

How to get the most out of this book

A brief chapter to help the reader get the most out of the day-by-day chapters.

Includes:

- How long it takes to work through the material.

- How to get the most out of each day's chapter.

- What you'll learn in Weeks Two, Three and Four.

- "Help! I can't complete the material in a week!" How to proceed if you can only work with the material on weekends.

- Confidence-builders, and encouragement for the reader to act on her ideas.

- Information on how to obtain a password and join the online forum for the book at the [Title Excerpted] Web site, and interact directly with the author.

Week One: Start Your New Business In Just Seven Days!

Introduction & Day One: Getting Started

The Introduction and Day One are included in the proposal, please see the Sample Chapters.

Day Two: your portfolio, prospecting and marketing

On Day Two, the reader takes the first steps in marketing her skills. She creates her bio, and begins to compile her portfolio, and writes a direct mail letter to sell her skills.

Includes:

- ✔ Copywriter's bio. The reader learns how to leverage her current experience and skills, and writes her first copywriter's bio. Her current experience and skills also show her which businesses she could begin targeting in her marketing. Includes sample bios. (I include sample bios written by my students – real-life student samples are included right throughout the book.)

- ✔ Copywriter's portfolio. The reader begins creating her copywriter's portfolio by creating writing samples. An explanation of an electronic portfolio.

- ✔ Market research. The reader learns how to find markets, and a prospecting routine is discussed in detail.

- ✔ First direct mail letter. The reader writes her first direct mail letter to send out to prospects; a sample letter is provided.

- ✔ Day Two copywriting techniques.

- ✔ Day Two Exercises.

Day Three: Writing Longer Copy

Day Three's theme is "news". The reader learns to write longer copy, including news releases and newsletters. She writes a news release for her new copywriting services business, and collects sample newsletters to study. She also learns the "Brain Dead" writing process, so that she can quickly write copy, to order, and to deadline.

Includes:

- ➢ News releases step-by-step. The reader learns to write a news release. She also targets media outlets to which she'll send her first news release.

- ➢ Publicity is better (and cheaper) than paid advertising, so the reader writes a news release for her new copywriting services business. A sample news release is provided.

- ➢ Newsletters are excellent promotional tools. The reader discovers the elements of a newsletter. A sample online newsletter is provided.

- ➢ Day Three copywriting techniques. Includes how to follow up on initial contact, and turn prospects into clients.

- ➢ Day Three Exercises.

Day Four: Public Relations Copywriting

In Day Four, the reader will become more comfortable with writing long copy PR, and develop skill creating and working with ideas. She'll price her services. She will also create a tagline (slogan) for her business.

Includes:

- ✔ Concepts and communications plans. The reader learns how to develop a concept and communications plan for a client with a new product or service.

- ✔ Pricing. The reader learns how to price her copywriting services.

- ✔ Day Four copywriting techniques. How to use incentives in copy. Create a Public Relations media kit: the reader discovers how to create a media kit for her new business, and for her clients. More on writing news releases --- how to avoid having a news release perceived as an ad.

- ✔ Sidebar: What should a copywriter know? A method for the reader to become comfortable writing the kinds of copy she's never written before.

- ➢ Day Four Exercises.

Day Five: Specialist Copywriting

In Day Five, the reader considers her past experience, and her interests, and considers building a copywriting specialty. The reader also learns to build her copywriting practice one client at a time, and how to use each client's circle of contacts to build her own contact base.

Includes:

- ➢ Copywriting specialization --- yes or no?

- ➢ Build a specialty in three easy steps.

- ➢ Networking and partnering with others. Copywriters who work completely alone limit themselves to small projects --- and a smaller income. The reader learns to become comfortable sub-contracting work like graphic design, and also how to work as a sub-contractor for others.

- ➢ Difficult clients. The reader learns to rely on her copywriting services agreement.

- ➢ Day five copywriting techniques. Add punch to copy. Find copywriting jobs online. Create a mini-proposal.

- ➢ Day Four Exercises.

Day Six: Focus on Marketing

In Day Six, the reader works on marketing her new business. The reader realizes the importance of marketing every day, and that all the marketing she does is cumulative. The reader creates a marketing plan. We discuss ten easy marketing tools.

Includes:

- ❐) Create a marketing plan for your copywriting business. Why creating a marketing plan is important, what to include in the plan. Regular review of the plan for what's working and what isn't.

- ❐) Ten marketing tools you can use. Includes: Internet job boards, building a Web site, writing promotional articles, and joining organizations.

- ❐) Day Six Exercises.

Day Seven: Copywriting for performance

In Day Seven, the reader discovers performance copywriting: writing for radio and television, and writing speeches and presentations, as well as writing for video and multimedia (CD-ROMs). Performance copywriting is a huge field.

Includes:

1. Conversational style. The importance of developing a natural, jargon-free, conversational style when writing for performance.

2. Video scripts, speeches and sales presentations.

3. Copywriting for radio and TV.

4. Copywriting how-to: writing radio spots; working with multimedia companies.

5. Day Seven Exercises.

Week Two: Your copywriting services marketing plan and more

In Week Two, the reader continues to build her business, by creating a more comprehensive marketing plan. She continues with the work of Week One, marketing her business.

Includes:

- ➤ More information on marketing.

> Marketing using online resources. The reader learns to build an "almost instant" Web site, which she can use as an online portfolio.

> The reader learns about pitching, and how presentations can build her business.

> Strategic alliances. The reader learns how to partner with other people like graphic designers so that she can target larger businesses.

Week Three: Copywriting for the Internet

In Week Three, the reader learns to write for the online environment. Includes:

1. Why writing for the Web is different from writing for print.
2. Various types of Web sites, and how to write copy for them.
3. Understanding a Web site's target audience.
4. How to write Web pages step by step.
5. Tips for the reader to market her copywriting services business online.

Week Four: Writing bios (biographies) and creating your own media kit

In Week Four, the reader will do more work on promoting her business. She will develop a media kit for her business.

This chapter includes a final section: "The end of this book; the beginning of your new life as a successful copywriter". This section is a final wrap-up, with some reminders, and encouragement and motivation for the reader.

Sample Chapters: Introduction and Day One

Introduction

Want to make REAL money writing?

You know you can write. Maybe you're even making money writing. But are you making enough money writing? Or is it just a hobby, costing you more in computers, postage and paper than you're earning? According to writers' organizations, 95 per cent of writers never make enough money to quit their day job.

What about the top five per cent of writers --- they're making big money, right? A small proportion of the top five per cent sure are. They're the headliners --- brand name writers like Stephen King and Dean Koontz. Journeymen (and women) writers are doing OK too. They're the genre writers, writing romance, mystery and suspense, and non-fiction. Writers in this group spend a lot of time looking over their shoulder. Will their publisher accept their next book? Are they writing enough? (Gotta turn in at least two books this year.) What nasty reviews of their latest book will they find on Amazon.com today? Magazine writers may do well too if they combine magazine writing with writing books.

If you want to make real money from your writing skills, you can. And you can do it easily and quickly, in seven days. How? Start a copywriting services business.

I've been making good money as a copywriter for over 25 years. It's fun, lucrative and creative.

Can YOU make money freelance copywriting?

Copywriters write for business. They write the words that educate, sell and instruct--- everyday words. The words on ads, leaflets, brochures, press releases, product instructions and labels, newsletters, direct mail, and on Web sites. These words are everywhere, and are invisible to most people. To copywriters, all these words indicate a market. Copywriters can make excellent money: the most experienced, enterprising, and productive copywriters scoop in a comfortable six figures annually.

There's nothing fancy or magical about the words copywriters produce. In fact, if you can write clear instructions or a letter, you can write copy. You don't have to be a great writer to be an excellent copywriter, but you do need to recognize and be able to use the attributes of both fiction (evoke emotion) and non-fiction (be clear) in your writing.

Of all the writing I do, I love copywriting most. It's fun, it's easy, it's creative --- and the biggest plus of all, it's usually short. Whatever writing you're currently doing, whether it's novels, short stories, or magazine articles, you'll feel at home with copywriting, and it will be an additional income stream for you. If you're a new writer, the skills you learn while writing copy easily transfer to other kinds of writing.

Here's the successful freelance copywriter's mindset. You:

- know that you're surrounded by copy every day, everywhere you look. Radio, TV, the Internet, newspapers, food product labels, signs: they all contain words, and a copywriter wrote them. To most people, copy is so ubiquitous it's invisible. To you, copy signals a market. You're observant and aware, and every time a message catches your eye, even if it's only a street sign, you're thinking: "Hmmm... a potential market";

- are interested in getting your client's message across;

- are prepared to market, and then market your services some more.

First must-do: get your client's message across

When you're writing copy, you're writing it for someone else, to do a specific job. That job may be to get someone to buy something, or to do something. In the case of a news release, you may be trying disseminate information or to change someone's opinion. Whatever you're writing, the message is the client's, and your job as copywriter is to make that message crystal clear.

If the copy fails --- and you won't need to look far to find poor copy --- it's because the copywriter failed to deliver the message. When I catch myself thinking about a print ad or a TV commercial: "Woeful writing"! I ask myself: "Did I get the message?" If the answer is "I have no idea what they're selling and I could care less", it's bad copy. On the other hand, if my answer is: "I hate everything about it, but I know what they're selling and what they want me to do", it's good copy.

Second must-do: market your copywriting services

There's a huge market for copywriting services. Every business uses copy. You may need to educate smaller businesses on what you can do for them, but the market is there. If you've tried to sell other kinds of writing, like novels or magazine articles, the openness of the copywriting market will come as a huge relief. It's not hard to find copywriting work.

However, you do need to market. As a group, we writers are not the world's hustlers. We're not pushy or extroverted. We'd rather write than sell our services by telemarketing or by appearing unannounced in a prospect's office.

Take heart. If you're by nature shy, you can make initial contact with clients via postal mail or e-mail, or by some other gentle, but resourceful method of self-promotion. You don't have to change your personality to find effective and fun ways to promote your services.

That's all it takes to make money freelance copywriting. Know that copy is everywhere and that it's all a market, get your client's message across, and market yourself.

How much can you earn?

It's no exaggeration to say that the sky's the limit on your earning potential as a copywriter. If you want to push your marketing, within a couple of years, you can be earning a six-figure income without breaking much of a sweat.

When you're just starting out, you'll charge somewhere between $50 and $100 an hour. As your experience grows, you'll charge more. If you have expertise in areas like finance, real estate, and multimedia, you can charge much more right away.

Of course, your hourly rate is not all gravy. You need to figure your expenses and overheads into that tally before you start to calculate the profits. But you can make money copywriting, a lot of money, because all businesses need to communicate and you're an expert communicator.

Welcome to the wonderful world of copy! Let's get started.

Day One: Getting Started

Your Day One Objectives

On Day One, you'll learn about the client brief, and will develop your own briefing sheet. You'll also learn a nifty technique to help you write copy anywhere, anytime.

Sections:

> ➢ The client brief.

> ➢ Writing copy step by step.

➢ How to Write A Perfect, Selling Ad.

➢ Day One Exercises.

The brief, and your Writing Services Agreement

In copywriting, you don't need to do it all yourself. In fact, you can't. Your copy is based on whatever you're trying to sell. This is a huge plus, because the product always gives you somewhere to start writing. And the more you know about the product, the better. Your client hands you the product, or tells you about it, or explains the service, or gives you a guided tour of the factory, and tells you what he wants: a sales letter, a brochure or a news release. This is "the brief", your instructions.

After he's explained the brief, the most important question to ask your client is: "What do you want the reader to do after he reads this?" (Or the viewer or listener to do, if you're writing broadcast copy or for a Web site.) You're asking what the customer's response should be. Getting the customer's response is your goal. The response could be: to call a phone number, to attend a sale, or to order from the catalog.

Write down the customers' required response. While I'm working on a job, I like to stick a reminder note onto my computer monitor: "Call client number", for example, or "order product". When you get into the excitement of writing the copy, your thoughts can get tangled. It's easy to forget the response. Writing the required response down, and keeping it visible, means that it's always at the forefront of your mind.

Your briefing sheet

If you've been hired by an agency, you'll be given a brief. If you're hired by a business unused to working with copywriters, you'll need to fill out your own briefing sheet. The sample briefing sheet below contains information that's useful to have. Tailor it to your own requirements. Computer-format your briefing sheet with adequate spacing so it's easy to fill in, then print out some copies and keep them by the phone.

SAMPLE BRIEFING SHEET (Figure 1)

Type of product or service:

Promotional name of the product or service:

Any other names?

A short description:

What three major points do you want to make?

What's the primary reason the customer would be interested in this product or service?

A technical description (or ask for the manufacturer's specification):

Options (colors, material etc):

Used for, and how?

Target audience:

Benefits over competing products:

Comments:

Customer response required:

Are there any disclaimers, or legal requirements which need to be mentioned in the copy?

Your Writing Services Agreement

ALWAYS SEND THE CLIENT YOUR WRITING SERVICES AGREEMENT, as soon as you accept the brief. Yes, it's in caps, and I'm shouting, and the reason is this: all the hassles you're likely to encounter during your copywriting career can be countered with an effective agreement, signed by the client, BEFORE you start work. Whenever I accept a brief, and omit this vital step, something goes wrong. So do it. Always. No exceptions.

When you're working as a sub-contractor with an agency, whether the agency is for advertising, Public Relations, or multimedia services, the agency will usually have its own agreement that you'll be asked to sign. Most agency agreements are straightforward. Sometimes they're not. Strike out anything in the agency agreement you don't agree with, initial your strikeouts, sign the agreement and send it back.

Here's the Writing Services Agreement I use. It's not fancy, but it does the job. Feel free to use it, or parts of it, to create your own agreement.

SAMPLE WRITING SERVICES AGREEMENT

(Figure 2.)

Agreement for Writing Services

REF: XXXX

DATE:

Client:

Project:

Fee:

Advance retainer:

Balance due on completion:

Notes:

Your signature below authorizes me to write copy for the project above, for the fee stated. (You can return the agreement via postal mail, fax, or e-mail.)

Two revisions are included if requested within five days of your receipt of copy, and are not based on a change in the assignment brief made after copy is submitted. Balance of payment is due on receipt of the invoice.

You understand that the assignment is work done for hire, which gives you the copyright. You release me from any responsibility for legal or regulatory problems that may arise from the use of any copy I write for you.

Payment options:

Check, Direct Deposit

(Sidebar) The copywriter's formula: AIDA

Memorize this. I don't know who to credit for this copywriting formula, but AIDA (Attract, Interest, Desire, Action) is a handy copy checklist. All the copy you write should include these elements.

Attract = get the reader's attention.

Interest = keep his attention.

Desire = evoke emotion.

Action = get a response.

Writing copy step by step

The more copy you write for clients each day, the more money you make. Therefore, you need a method to get copy written fast, without dithering and wasting time wondering what to do next. The following method works. I recommend that you use it on every job. More play than work, it's fun and stress-free. Try it.

Step One: Research

After you've been briefed by the client, your first step is research. Even if you're sure that you have all the information you need, doing a bit of hunting and gathering for more information lets your subconscious mind brood on the task before you start writing.

My aim when I research is always to get what I call "the Click". The Click is part concept, part inspiration, part structure, and part my subconscious mind waving at me and yelling: "Yoohoo! We're ready, you can get started."

Your research period may be only a few minutes. When I was asked to do a fast rewrite job on five 30-second radio spots for a jewellery store, out of the two hours I had, I spent half an hour on research. Although I'd worked for the client previously, and knew what he was selling, I wanted to get a new angle, a unique fact – something different that I could base the copy around. I found it. I learned that gold is eternal: it's older than our solar system. That nugget of info inspired me, and let me breeze through writing the five spots.

Unless I'd been prepared to "waste" time on the research, I would have had a much harder time writing the copy, and the copy wouldn't have had any creative sparkle.

Step Two: Prepare by getting a conversation down on paper or on the computer screen

The biggest stumbling block for a writer is the blank page or computer screen. Writers get performance anxiety just like actors get stage fright. Luckily, that block is easy to conquer when you're writing copy.

Copy is conversational. If you're used to writing novels or non-fiction, this can be hard to achieve at first. Good copy is simply communication, rather than literary elegance, and you don't have to agonize over grammar. If you're getting your client's message across, you're writing good copy.

Here's a handy trick to get words on the page. When you start writing, imagine you're talking to someone, telling her about the product. It helps to type something like: "Jeannie, I just found this great new thing, let me tell you about it..." Then describe the product.

Or, if you're writing longer copy, longer than a typical page of 250 words, talk into a tape recorder, and pretend to tell someone about the product, then transcribe the tape. Either of these techniques will stop you using a stiff and formal voice. You'll be using an informal conversational style and tone, which is appropriate for copy.

You'll also notice you've conquered the blank page.

Step Three: Brainstorm with word associations

You've got a page of conversation. Print it out if it's on the computer. Without thinking about it too much, circle any words which appeal to you. Circle five words. At this stage, you're nowhere near writing the final copy. You're making creative connections. This method of brainstorming uses your right and left brain.

Starting with the first word, write down 20 word associations you come up with. You can use a cluster diagram, or just make a list.

The key to getting results with this method is lack of effort on your part. Just do the process mechanically, and write down the first words which pop into your mind.

When you've done this, go and do something else for a while. Have a cup of coffee, or take the dog for a walk. Sometimes you'll get a rush job, and you won't be able to take much time away, but no matter how rushed you are, take at least ten minutes.

Step Four: First draft: write it fast

When you sit down at your desk, write a first draft as quickly as you can. Don't refer to any of the word lists you made. Be casual, be confident, and get those words down.

Your first draft is your first take on the job. This gives you something to work with, and you can tweak it until you're satisfied.

As you become more experienced, your first draft comes close to being your final draft. I usually send my second draft to the client as the "Initial Draft". I offer two free revisions of this draft in my writing agreement. I've found that if I'm working for the client directly, then either the client accepts my Initial Draft, and says "Great! Just what I want", or I do one minor revision. When working with an agency, I rarely get asked to do revisions.

My feeling is that because I've done a lot of preparation (research, getting a conversation down, and brainstorming), I'm pretty much on target when I send the Initial Draft. Therefore, the preparation work you do is important. Don't try to jump into a final draft that you intend to send to the client when you sit down at the computer. You'll freeze up. Having a process that you work through leaves plenty of room for discovery ---and all writing is discovery --- and creativity, and this shows in the final results. Even if you don't use any of the material you created in your preparation in the final draft, the preparation process loosens you up and helps you to write creative copy day after day, because you're not working --- you're playing, and your subconscious mind loves to play.

Copywriter's How –To: Five Easy Tips To Write A Perfect, Selling Ad

(Each chapter contains Copywriter's How-Tos, copywriting reference articles.)

A perfect, selling ad? I lied. There's no such animal as the perfect, works-every-time, selling ad. But I got you to read this far, didn't I? That was the title's purpose --- see Tip Two: Write an attention-grabbing headline.

I didn't lie about these tips, though. They're easy and fun to use.

Tip One: who's the reader? (Or viewer, or listener if you're writing for broadcast.)

Although you're writing for a crowd, it's easiest to write if you imagine you're talking to one particular person.

You can even start writing your first draft with a salutation, as if you were writing a letter: Start with "Dear Elli", and keep writing.

Who is this person? Is she old, young, married? Where does she live? What's her life like? What does she want most? What's she scared of? Why would she be interested in your product? What difference would it make in her life?

Professional copywriters spend a lot of time in this phase of the writing process. You can't motivate someone if you don't know who they are.

Tip Two: Write an attention-grabbing headline

Your headline is vital. No one is looking for your ad. You've got to wave and yell at them to get their attention. If you don't get their attention, no sale.

Write a trial headline to get yourself started. This probably won't be the headline you'll use. However, with a trial headline, you've got a corral for your copy. You're writing to that headline.

When you've written a draft of the ad, force yourself, with a timer, to write another twenty headlines in five minutes. (Read the rest of the tips and write the benefits and the response before you write a draft.)

Don't try too hard. Who cares if they're all junk? You're writing lots of headlines to get your subconscious mind to take you seriously, and throw up the PERFECT headline. You'll never achieve this perfect headline with conscious thought. It's a gift from your subconscious, but you have to goose it into cooperating.

You may find a headline you like more than your initial headline. Just substitute it, if it fits. If it doesn't you can write another version of the ad to fit that headline's concept.

Tip Three: Write the features first, then work out what the benefits are

Nobody buys a product (or a service) for its own sake. They buy because it benefits them in some way. The benefits are what you're selling.

- You're not selling a German Shepherd puppy, you're selling an intelligent, loyal companion and family protector.

- You're not selling a car, you're selling travelling comfort, prestige, and a sure-fire babe-magnet.

- You're not selling a book, you're selling the adventure of a lifetime, love, romance, and sex.

To get a handle on this, take a sheet of paper and briefly list the features of your product or service on the left.

Then beside the feature, write the corresponding benefit that each feature provides.

Remember --- use the benefits in your ad.

Tip Four: Don't forget the response!

I've lost count of the number of ads I've seen everywhere from the Yellow Pages to full display ads costing thousands in magazines, where the copywriter and everyone else forgot the response.

You must tell the reader what you want him to do. You must ask for the sale. Ask the reader to do something: call a number, come into the store, go to a Web site.

This is so important that when I'm writing an ad I always write the required response on a sticky note and tape it to a corner of my monitor. I tape it onto the screen itself, so I can't miss it. (Yes, I have been guilty of forgetting the response. And very embarrassing it was too.)

Tip Five: Read it out loud

You've finished the final draft of your ad. Before you show it to anyone else, read it aloud.

You'll pick up redundancies, awkward sentence construction and other nasties when you read the copy aloud.

....

Bonus

Get No-Charge Access to Writing and Publishing Materials from Our Library Collection

Instant Access - Join Here

Click or type into your browser:

http://livesensical.com/go/writingbooks/

www.ingramcontent.com/pod-product-compliance
Lightning Source LLC
Chambersburg PA
CBHW022134170526
45157CB00004B/1874